BEYOND THE SONNET

120+ poetry options

Stephanie Neilan

Cartoon of William Shakespeare holding a feather quill and a scroll by Krisdog, Deposit photo ID: 102670738

Poems are about expression. The rules don't matter as much as the feelings. For this reason, new poems, with new definitions and rules, are constantly being created as variations of traditional poems are explored. This collection includes over 120 different poetry forms. (And that's after I excluded ones based primarily on theme!) Some sites I pulled from while compiling my list included shadowpoetry.com, writersdigest.com, poetryfoundation.org, and poets.org. Whether you choose to rhyme and have a specific meter for your poem or not, there is a poetry style out there to justify your choice.

<u>Some poem styles removed due to their thematic emphasis</u>
Clerihew – humorous
Pastoral – nature
Epulaeryu - food
Christ in a Rhyme - religion
Memento – a memory/anniversary
Epitaph – Tombstone
Elegy – About the death of a loved one
Burlesque – Humor in a serious subject
Allegory – uses extensive allegories
Image – devoted to creating images in your mind when you read it
Parallelogram – a poem that compares a loved one to nature.

Alphabetical Listing

-ing
A L'Arora
Abecedarian
Abstract
Acrostic (see Abecedarian)
Alliterisen
Alouette
Alphabet Poetry
American Sentence
Anagrammatic Poetry
Ballad (see Narrative)
Ballade
Blank Verse
Blitz
Blues Poem
Bop
Bref Double
Brevette
Cascade
Catalogue (see List)
Cento (see Found Poem)
Chant
CinqTroisDecaLa Rhyme
Cinquain
Clarity Pyramid
Concrete (see Shape)
Compound Word Verse
Con-Verse
Constanza
Couplet
Decuain
Diamante
Diatelle

Lune
Madrigal
Memoriam
Mini-Monoverse
Minute Poetry
Mirror Sestet
Mirrored Refrain
Monchielle
Monorhyme
Monotetra
Musette
Naani
Narrative
Nonet
Nove Otto
Octameter
Oddquain
Ode (Horatian, Pindaric, Irregular)
Ottava Rima
Palindrome
Pantoum
Paradelle
Pleiades
Prose Poem
Puente
Quadrilew
Quatern
Quatrain
Quinzaine
Renga
Rhyme Royal
Rictameter
Riddle Poem
Rispetto
Rondeau
Rondel

Rondelet
Roundabout
Sedoka (see Katauta)
Senryu (see Haiku)
Sapphic
Septolet
Sestina
Shadorma
Shape
Sijo
Sonnet, Canzone
Sonnet, Italian and English
Somonka (see Tanka)
Sound (see Abstract)
Synchronicity
Tanka
Terza Rima
Terzanelle
Tetractys
Tongue Twister
Tri-fall
Triolet
Triquain
Triquint
Triversen
Trochee
Trois-par-Huit
Tyburn
Vers Beaucoup
Villanelle
Wrapped Refrain

Poems and Their Definitions

-ing

A poem where the title is a word or short sentence. The rest of the poem consists of words ending in "-ing" that describe it.

A L'Arora

A collection of at least four, eight-lined stanzas that have the rhyme scheme abcdefgf.

Abecedarian (Acrostic)

Sometimes called acrostic, this is a poem where specific letters of the lines, usually the first letters, form a word or message relating to the subject.

Abstract (Sound)

Also known as a sound poem, it uses the ways words sound to convey meaning and emotion more than the word itself.

Alliterisen

A seven-lined poem with two alliterations per line. The first line has "x" (any number that is used consistently to mean x throughout the poem) syllables, the second line has "x" plus two syllables. The third line has "x" minus one syllable. The fourth line has "x" plus one syllable. The fifth line has "x"-2 syllables, and the sixth and seventh lines have "x" number of syllables.

Alouette

A collection of two or more stanzas of six lines each. The syllable count per line is five, five, seven, five, five, seven, and the rhyme scheme is aabccb.

Alphabet Poetry

A poem where every letter of the alphabet is used as the first letter of a word in the poem (minimum 26 words).

American Sentence

A line of poetry that is 17 syllables long.

Anagrammatic Poetry

A poem created from words using letters from the title. (No other letters!)

Ballade

The ballade contains three main stanzas, each with the same rhyme scheme, plus a shorter concluding stanza, or envoi. All four stanzas have identical final refrain lines.

Blank Verse

Unrhymed lines of iambic (an unstressed syllable followed by a stressed syllable) pentameter (10 syllables/line).

Blitz

A 50-lined poem. Line one should be one short phrase or image (like "I can fly"). Line two should be another short phrase or image using the same first word as the first word in line one (something like "I can float"). Lines three and four should be short phrases or images using the last word of line two as their first words (so line three might be "Float at home" and line four might be "Float at sea"). Lines five and six should be short phrases or images using the last word of line four as their first words, and so on until you've made it through 48 lines. Line 49 should be the last word of line 48 and line 50 should be the last word of line 47. The title of the poem should be three words long. The first word of the title is the first word of line 3, the second word is a preposition or conjunction, and the third word is the first word of line 47. There should be no punctuation.

Blues Poem

A three-lined poem that makes a statement in the first line, a variation in the second line, and an ironic alternative in the third line.

Bop

A 20-lined poem consisting of three stanzas. Each stanza is followed by a repeated line, or refrain, and each stanza undertakes a different purpose in the overall argument of the poem. The first stanza (six lines long) states the problem, and the second stanza (eight lines long) explores or expands upon the problem. If there is a resolution to the problem, the third stanza (six lines long) finds it. If there is no solution, then this final stanza talks about the attempt and failure to succeed. In addition to the three-stanza bop, some have added a six-line fourth stanza, still ending on the refrain.

Bref Double

A 14-lined poem divided into three quatrains (a four-lined stanza) and one couplet (a two-lined stanza) with three rhymes (an A rhyme, B rhyme, and C rhyme). The A and B rhymes appear twice in the first three stanzas and once each in the couplet. The C rhyme is the final line in each of the quatrains. For example, axbc xaxc xbxc ab or axxc bxxc abxc ab (x indicates a word that doesn't have to rhyme). The syllables are consistent, but not preset to a specific amount.

Brevette

A three-lined, three-word poem consisting of a noun, a verb, and a noun. In that order. Often times, the verbs have spaces between the letters to emphasize the word. For example, ooze would look like o o z e.)

Cascade

For the cascade poem, a poet takes each line from the first stanza of a poem and makes those the final lines of each stanza afterward. For example, a cascade poem based on a tercet would look like ABC / abA / cdB / efC, and a quatrain cascade would look like ABCD / abcA / defB / ghiC / jklD with capital letters indicating repeated lines.

Chant

A poem than uses repetitive lines to form a chant. The repetitive lines are often repeated every line or every other line and are more methodically done than a simple refrain.

CinqTroisDecaLa Rhyme

A ten-lined poem with 15 syllables on each line. The rhyme scheme is aabbcccabc

Cinquain

A five-lined, non-rhyming poem with one word on the top line, two on the second line, three on the third, four on the fourth, and one on the last. Another version of this poem limits its syllables instead with two syllables on the first line, four syllables on the second line, six syllables on the third, eight syllables on the fourth, and two syllables on the fifth.

Clarity Pyramid

A seven-lined poem divided into two triplets (three-lined poems) followed by a single line. The first triplet has one syllable in the first line, two syllables in the second line, and three syllables in the third line. The first line is also the title and is presented in all caps. The second and third lines clarify the meaning or are synonyms of the title. The second triplet has five syllables in the first line, six syllables in the second line, and seven syllables in the third line. It shows the first triplet in action. The last line is a quote, eight syllables long, that defines the title.

Compound Word Verse

A 15-lined poem divided into five, three-lined stanzas. The last line of each stanza ends with a compound word that shares a common stem word which is taken from the title. For example, if the title was "Snow" then an associated compound word could be something like snowflake, snowball, or snowshoe. The rhyme scheme is aab / ccd / eef / ggh / iij, and the syllable count per stanza is eight syllables in the first line, eight syllables in the second line, and three syllables in the last line.

Con-Verse

A collection of three or more rhyming couplets. Each couplet has the same number of syllables per line that increases by one for each verse. For example, if stanza one had a rhyme scheme of aa and seven syllables per line, then stanza two would have rhyme scheme bb and eight syllables per line. The syllable count increases until there are 11 syllables per line. It then skips back down to a syllable count of seven and restarts the count from there.

Constanza

A collection of five or more three-lined stanzas of eight syllables apiece. The first lines of all the stanzas could form their own poem, but the other lines add extra meaning. The rhyme scheme is abb / acc / add / aee / aff, etc.

Couplet

Two lines of poetry that may be rhymed or unrhymed.

Decuain

A ten-lined poem written in iambic pentameter (ten syllables per line that alternate between stressed and unstressed syllables, starting with an unstressed syllable). Its rhyme scheme is ababbcbcaa, ababbcbcbb, or ababbcbccc.

Diamante

A seven lined, non-rhyming poem with a word count that increases by one from one to four for the first four lines, and then decreases from three to one for the last three lines. (One word - two words - three words - four words - three words - two words- one word). The first word and the last word are opposite in nature. The first half of the poem is related to the first word, and the second half is about the last word. The second and sixth lines have two adjectives, and the third and fifth lines have three words ending in "-ing." In the fourth line, the first two words are about the first word in the poem, and the last two words are about the last word of the poem.

Diatelle

A 15-lined poem with a specific syllable count per line (one syllable on the first line, two syllables on the second line, three syllables on the third line, four syllables on the fourth, six syllables on the fifth, eight syllables on the sixth, ten syllables on the seventh, 12 syllables on the eighth, ten syllables on the ninth, eight syllables on the tenth, six syllables on the eleventh, four syllables on the twelfth, three syllables on the thirteenth, two syllables on the fourteenth, and one syllable on the last line). The rhyme scheme goes abbcbccaccbcbba.

Doggerel

A poem dominated by clichés, clumsiness, and irregular meter. It is often unintentionally humorous.

Duo-Rhyme

A 10 or 12-lined poem with the first two and last two lines having the same rhyme scheme, and the center of the poem having its own rhyme. Each line has eight beats of iambic measure (an unstressed syllable followed by a stressed syllable – 16 syllables total). An example rhyme scheme would be aabbbbbbaa.

Echo, Loop

A poem where the last word or syllable in a line is repeated or echoed underneath in the next line. If you restrict it to a four-lined stanza and make the rhyme scheme abcb, then it is called a loop poem.

Epigram

An epigram is a short, pithy saying, usually in verse, that often comes with a quick, satirical twist at the end.

Etheree

A ten-lined poem with a syllable count of one syllable in the first line, two on the second, then three, four, five, six, seven, eight, nine, and finally ten syllables on the tenth line. If you string more than one together, then you have to reverse the syllable count each time. For example, a triple etheree's syllable count would have one on the first line, two on the second, then three, four, five, six, seven, eight, nine, ten, ten, nine, eight, seven, six, five, four, three, two, one, one, two, three, four, five, six, seven, eight, nine, and then ten.

Fibonacci

A six-lined poem with one syllable on the first line, one syllable on the second line, then two on the third, three on the fourth, five on the fifth, and eight on the sixth.

Five Ws

A poem that answers the questions of who, what, when, where, and why.

Florette

A two-lined poem with six syllables apiece that have both an end rhyme and internal rhyme. A longer variation includes an aabba rhyme scheme, and an eight, eight, eight, eight, twelve syllable count with an iambic beat (an unstressed syllable followed by a stressed syllable).

Found Poem, Cento, Erasure

Found poems take existing texts and refashion them into poems, a literary equivalent of a collage. If its text comes exclusively from other poets, then that specific found poem is called a cento. If you create it by "erasing" portions of an existing poem/story/speech, then it is called an erasure.

Free Verse

No rules! It doesn't have to rhyme, have any sort of meter, or be about anything in particular. Just write what you feel.

Ghazal

A collection of five to 15 couplets that could be enjoyed on their own. Each line of the poem must be the same number of syllables. The first couplet rhymes and ends on a refrain. Subsequent couplets repeat the refrain in the second line, rhyming it with the first couplet. The final couplet usually includes the poet's signature, referring to the author in the first or third person, frequently including the poet's own name or a derivation of its meaning.

Golden Shovel

A poem that begins by taking a line (or lines) from another poem. The words in the line (or lines) become the end words of the golden shovel. If you use a line with six words, then your poem would be six lines long. If you use a stanza with 24 words, then your poem would be 24 lines long. The beginning words must be kept in the original order, and credit given to the poet who wrote the original line (or lines). The new poem does not have to be about the same subject as the original poem.

Grá Reformata

A poem with the rhyming structure of a villanelle, but with an extra couplet inserted between every tercet until the last seven lines. Written in iambic meter (an unstressed followed by a stressed syllable), the rhyme scheme goes abaxxabaxxabaxxabaxxabaabaa (x stands for the lines that don't have to rhyme).

Gwawdodyn

A poem composed of quatrains (4-line stanzas) that have a nine, nine, ten, nine syllable pattern per quatrain and matching end rhymes on lines 1, 2, and 4. One version has an internal rhyme within the third line. The second version has an internal rhyme within the third line that rhymes with an internal rhyme in the fourth line. Here's a possible diagram for the first version (with the x's symbolizing syllables): 1-xxxxxxxxa 2-xxxxxxxxa 3-xxxxbxxxxb 4-xxxxxxxxa. The second version might look like 1-xxxxxxxxa 2-xxxxxxxxa 3-xxxxbxxxxb 4-xxbxxbxxa.

Haiku, Haiga, Haibun, Senryu

A 3-lined, non-rhyming poem with five syllables in the first line, seven syllables in the second line, and five syllables in the third line. Haikus have a nature theme so if it's not about nature, then it is called a Senryu. A haiga is a haiku accompanied by a picture. A haibun is a haiku accompanied by a thematically connected prose poem.

Harrisham Rhyme

A six-lined rhyming stanza (ababab). The last letter of the first word of each line is the first letter of the first word of next line.

Hay(na)ku

Hay(na)ku is a three-lined poem with one word in the first line, two words in the second, and three in the third.

Hexsonnetta

A 14-lined poem consisting of two, six-lined stanzas with a finishing rhyming couplet in iambic meter (an unstressed syllable followed by an stressed one). The rhyme scheme is abbaab / cddccd / ee.

Joseph's Star

A collection of one or more, eight-lined stanzas made with one syllable on the first line, three on the second, five on the third, seven on the fourth and fifth lines, five on the sixth, three on the seventh, and one on the eighth.

Katauta, Sedoka

An unrhymed, three-lined poem with five syllables on the first line, seven syllables on line two, and seven syllables on line three. If you combine two katuatas together that are about the same subject but look at it from different perspectives, then it's called a sedoka. For example, if the theme was hunting then a katauta from the perspective of the hunter would be combined with one from the view point of the prey.

Kenning

A poem composed of two-word descriptions about the topic.

Kyrielle

A collection of four-lined stanzas that have a refrain in the fourth line. Often, there is a rhyme scheme in the poem like aabb, abab, aaab, or abcb.

La Charta

A collection of at least three six-lined stanzas that have eight syllables in iambic meter (unstressed syllables followed by stressed syllables) per line. The rhyme scheme is aaaabb / ccccdd / eeeeff.

La'ritmo

A 32-lined poem divided into quatrains (four-lined stanzas) with 12 syllables per line. The rhyme scheme is aabB / ccbB / ddbB / eefF / ggfF/ hhfF / iibB / jjfF (The last line of the first stanza, B, becomes the lines for the other Bs. At a minimum, the same ending word is used. The same rule applies to F for its stanzas.)

Lai

A nine-lined poem with a aabaabaab rhyme scheme and a syllable count of five, five, two, five, five, two, five, five, two.

Lanturne

A five-lined poem with one syllable on the first line, two in the second, three on the third, four on the fourth, and one on the fifth.

Lauranelle

A 22-lined poem in iambic meter (unstressed syllables followed by stressed syllables) – ten syllables per line. The rhyme scheme is A1bA2bcbcdcdedefefbfggA1A2 where the first and third lines are repeated as the last two lines.

Lento

An eight-lined poem divided into two quatrains (four-lined poems) with a rhyme scheme of abcb / defe or abab / cdcd. Additionally, the FIRST words of each stanza should rhyme with each other.

Limerick

A five-lined poem where the first line explains the situation, the second tells what happened, the third and fourth tell what went wrong, and the fifth tell the significance, the "so what". With "–" representing unstressed syllables and "/" representing stressed syllables, the meter is: (line one) -/--/--/, (line two) -/--/--/, (line three) -/--/, (line four) -/--/, and (line five) -/--/--/.

List (Catalogue)

Also called a catalogue poem, it's a poetical collection of lists (names, places, actions, thoughts, images, etc.).

Luc Bat

A poem consisting of alternating lines of six and eight syllables. The rhyming words are inserted into the syllable count so the layout of the poem (with x representing a syllable) looks like xxxxxa xxxxxaxb xxxxxb xxxxxbxc xxxxxc xxxxxcxd xxxxxd xxxxxdxe.

Lune

A 13-syllable poem that has five syllables in the first line, three syllables in the second line, and five syllables in the final line. A variation of the poem uses words instead of syllables with three words in the first line, five words in the second line, and three lines in the last line.

Madrigal

A poem composed of smaller stanzas. The Italian madrigal has 2-3 tercets (three-lined stanzas) followed by 1-2 couplets (two-lined stanzas) with seven or eleven syllables per line. The English version is written in iambic pentameter (10 syllables alternating between stressed and unstressed syllables and beginning with the unstressed one.) It has a tercet (three-lined stanza), a quatrain (four-lined stanza), and a sestet (six-lined stanza). With capital letters indicating repeated lines, the rhyme scheme looks like A,B1,B2 / a,b,A,B1 / a,b,b,A,B1,B2.

Memoriam

A quatrain in iambic tetrameter (eight syllables total that alternate between stressed and unstressed syllables and beginning with the unstressed one) with a rhyme scheme of abba.

Mini-Monoverse

A ten-line poem broken into two, 5-lined stanzas, 3 syllables per line. Each stanza has its own monorhyme (aaaaa / bbbbb). Ideally, it tells a story.

Minute Poetry

A 12-lined rhyming poem in iambic meter (an unstressed
syllable followed by a stressed syllable) with 60 syllables
total. Divided into three stanzas of four lines each, there are
eight syllables in the first line, four syllables in line two,
four syllables in line three, and four syllables in line four.
The rhyme scheme is aabb / ccdd / eeff.

Mirror Sestet

A poem consisting of one or more six-lined stanzas. The
first word of line one rhymes with the last word of line one.
The first word of line two is the last word of line one and
the last word of line two is the first word of line one. The
first word of line three rhymes with the last word of line
three. The first word of line four is the last word of line
three and the last word of line four is the first word of line
three. The first word of line five rhymes with the last word
of line five. The first word of line six is the last word of
line five, and the last word of line six is the first word of
line five. The Mirror Sestet can also be written in non-
rhyme, but all other rules must be followed.

Mirrored Refrain

A poem of three or more quatrains with alternating refrains.
With x indicating a non-rhyming word and capital letters
indicating a repeated line, the rhyme scheme looks like
xaBA, xbAB, xaBA, xbAB.

Monchielle

A 20-lined poem broken into four, five-lined stanzas where
the first line repeats in each verse with six syllables per
line. The rhyme pattern is Abcdc / Aefgf / Ahiji / Aklml.

Monorhyme

A poem where the end words of each line rhyme together.

Monotetra

A poem where each quatrain (four-lined stanza) has its own monorhyme. Each line is eight syllables long, and the last line of each stanza repeats the first four syllables on that line as its last four syllables.

Musette

A nine-lined poem that consists of three stanzas of three lines each. The syllable count goes two, four, two / two, four, two / two, four, two, and the rhyme scheme is aba / cdc / efe.

Naani

A four-lined poem consisting of 20-25 syllables total.

Narrative, Epic, Ballad

A narrative poem about the adventures and bravery of a hero. If it is sung, it's called a ballad. If it's really long, then it's called an epic poem.

Nonet

A nine-lined poem that has nine syllables in the first line, eight in the second, seven in the third, six on the fourth, five on the fifth, four on the sixth, three on the seventh, two on the eight, and one on the ninth.

Nove Otto

A nine-lined poem with eight syllables per line. The rhyme scheme is aacbbcddc.

Octameter

A 16-lined poem divided into two stanzas of eight lines each with five syllables per line. The rhyme scheme is abcdedfd / ghcgigdd.

Oddquain

A five-lined, non-rhyming poem with one syllable on the first line, three on the second, five on the third, seven on the fourth, and one on the fifth.

Ode (Horatian, Pindaric, Irregular)

A long, elaborate, lyrical poem. Horatian odes are written in two or four-lined stanzas, each with the same metrical pattern. Pindaric odes are ceremonious poems consisting of a strophe (two or more lines repeated as a unit performed when the reader would move across the stage) followed by an antistrophe (stanza read when the reader would move back to their original spot) with the same metrical pattern and concluding with an epode (a summary line said from the original spot) in a different meter. Irregular odes are irregular in verse and structure and lack a feeling of correspondence between the parts.

Ottava Rima

A collection of eight-lined stanzas with ten or eleven syllables per line. The rhyme scheme is abababcc.

Palindrome

A poem that can be read backward and forward (like the word "race car"). It can be done with letters, but also with words.

Pantoum

A poem composed of four-line stanzas in which the second and fourth lines of each stanza serve as the first and third lines of the next stanza. The last line of a pantoum is often the same as the first.

Paradelle

A four-stanza poem. Each stanza consists of six lines. For
the first three stanzas, the first and second lines should be
the same, the third and fourth lines should also be the same,
and the fifth and sixth lines should take the words from the
first four lines (and only those words) and rearrange them
into two new lines. The final stanza is created using the
words from fifth and sixth lines of the first three stanzas
and only the words from the fifth and sixth lines of the first
three stanzas.

Pleiades

A seven-lined poem where each line begins with the first
letter of the poem's single-word title. For example, if the
title was Hello, then all the lines in the poem would begin
with H. A variation of this poem requires limiting the
length to six syllables per line.

Prose Poem

A poem that looks like prose but reads like poetry.

Puente

A poem with two stanzas connected by a "bridge." The
bridge is a single line of poetry that can be read at the end
of the first stanza or the beginning of the second stanza and
is usually marked by a tilde (~). The exact number of lines
and syllables is up to you. The two halves of the poem
should be related, but different.

Quadrilew

A 16-lined poem divided in quatrains that rotate between
five and six syllables per line (Poets can choose to start on
either the five or the six count). The rhyme scheme is
a,B1,A2,B2 / B1,c,b,c / A2,d,a,d / B2,e,b,e with capital
letters representing repeating lines.

Quatern

A 16-lined poem composed of four four-lined stanzas. Each line is eight syllables long. It doesn't have to rhyme, but you do have to repeat the first line throughout the poem so the set up looks like Abcd / eAfg / hiAj/ klmA. (Capital A represents the repeating line.)

Quatrain

A four-lined poem that traditionally utilizes some sort of rhyme scheme.

Quinzaine

A three-lined, 15 syllable poem with seven syllables in the first line, five in the second, and three in the third. The first line makes a statement, and the next two ask questions related to that statement.

Renga

A poem created by two or more poets. One poet writes the first stanza, which divides 17 syllables over three lines. The next poet adds the second stanza, a couplet with seven syllables per line. The third stanza repeats the structure of the first and the fourth repeats the second, alternating in this pattern until the poem's end.

Rhyme Royal

A seven-lined poem in iambic pentameter (ten syllables that alternate between stressed and unstressed syllables, beginning with the unstressed syllable) with a rhyme scheme of ababbcc. Multiple Rhyme royals may be strung together.

Rictameter

A nine-lined poem with two syllables on the first line, four on the second, six on the third, then eight, ten, eight, six, four, and finally two syllables on the last line.

Riddle Poem

A five-lined poem. The first line gives a clue about the subject. The second line has an adjective and a noun related to the word. The third line has two actions connected to the subject. The fourth line has a phrase or statement, and line five gives the answer to the riddle.

Rispetto

An eight-lined poem. Option one divides the lines into two quatrains written in iambic (unstressed followed by an stressed) tetrameter (four "feet"– eight syllables). Option two has the lines written as a single stanza with hendecasyllabic (11-syllable) lines. The rhyme scheme for both is either ababccdd or abababcc.

Rondeau

A 15-lined poem, eight to ten syllables each, divided into a quintet (five-lined stanza), a quatrain (four-lined stanza), and a sestet (six-lined stanza). With R representing the first few words or the entire first line of the first stanza, the rhyme scheme is aabba / aabR / aabbaR.

Rondel

A 13-lined poem divided into three stanzas, usually eight syllables per line. The rhyme scheme is ABba / abAB / abbaA (uppercase letters represent repeated lines or refrains). A rondel prime, sometimes called rondel supreme, adds a 14th line to the poem. (ABba / abAB / abbaAB)

Rondelet

A seven-lined poem with two rhymes and one refrain. With capital letters indicating repeated lines, the rhyme scheme goes AbAabbA. The refrain (A) is four to five syllables long, and the rest of the lines are twice as long (eight or ten syllables).

Roundabout

A 20-lined poem divided into four stanzas of five lines each. It has an iambic meter (unstressed followed by a stressed syllable), and eight syllables for the first line, six for the second, four for the third, four for the fourth, and six for the fifth line. The rhyme scheme is abccb / bcddc / cdaad / dabba.

Sapphic

A four-lined poem with a specific meter. The first three lines are two trochees (stressed syllable, "/", followed by an unstressed syllable, "-"), a dactyl (/--), and then two more trochees, or /-/-/--/-/-. The fourth line is a dactyl followed by a trochee, /--/-. Alternately, two stressed syllables could replace both the second and last foot (trochee or dactyl) of each line.

Septolet

A 14-word, seven-lined poem that is divided into two parts. Both parts deal with the same event/thought/moment but from different perspectives.

Sestina

A 39-lined poem that repeats the initial six end-words of the first stanza through the remaining five six-lined stanzas, ending in a three-line envoi. With capital letters to represent the ending words, the order of the words is ABCDEF for the first stanza, FAEBDC for the second stanza, CFDABE for the third stanza, ECBFAD for the fourth, DEACFB for the fifth, and BDFECA for the sixth. The envoi, seventh stanza, is either ECA or ACE. The envoi must also include the remaining three end-words, BDF, so that all six recurring words appear in the final three lines.

Shadorma

A six-lined poem with syllables spread out so three are on the first line, five on the second, three on the third, three on the fourth, seven on the fifth, and five on the sixth.

Shape (concrete)

Sometimes called a concrete poem, it takes the shape of what the poem represents.

Sijo

A three-lined poem averaging 14-16 syllables per line (for a poem total of 44-46 syllables). Line one introduces the situation, line two develops the theme, and line three concludes with a "twist" of meaning, sound, etc. Each line has a "break" or pause somewhere in the middle.

Sonnet, Canzone

A seven to 20-lined rhyming poem broken into six stanzas with a shorter ending stanza (seven stanzas total) and 10-11 syllables per line. (The rhyme scheme is not specified.)

Sonnet, Italian and English

14-lined poem in iambic pentameter (ten syllables that alternate between stressed and unstressed syllables, beginning with an unstressed one). The Italian sonnet rhyme scheme is (abbaabba / cdecde / aa or abbaabba / cdccdc / aa). The English (Shakespearian) version has three quatrains (four-lined stanzas) with a concluding couplet.

Synchronicity

A 24-lined, non-rhyming poem divided into eight, three-line stanzas. Each stanza has eight syllables in the first line, eight in the second, and two in the third. It is usually written in first person with a twist in the last two stanzas.

Tanka, Somonka

A five-lined, thirty-one-syllable poem with five syllables on the first line, seven on the second, five on the third, and seven on the last two lines. Alternatively, it can be written as a single line of poetry. If you have two tankas that connect to each other, then it is called a somonka.

Terza Rima

A group of tercets (three-lined stanzas) that are united by using the second line to rhyme with the first and third lines of the following tercet so the rhyme scheme looks like aba / bcb / cdc / ded, etc.

Terzanelle

A 19-lined poem with five tercets (three-lined stanzas) and one quatrain (four-lined stanza). With capital letters indicating repeating lines, the rhyme scheme looks like ABA / bCB / cDC / dED / eFE / fAFA or ABA / bCB / cDC / dED / eFE / fFAA. Each line should have the same number of syllables.

Tetractys

A five-lined poem with one syllable on the first line, two on the second, three on the fourth, then four on the fourth, and ten on the last line. The syllable count can also be reversed with ten syllables on the first line and one syllable on the last one. If you combine multiple tetractys together, then you alternate between increasing and decreasing the syllable count.

Tongue Twister

A poem that capitalizes on the use of similar sounding words. (Think of "Fuzzy Wuzzy")

Tri-fall

An 18-lined poem divided into three six-line stanzas. The rhyme scheme for each stanza is abcabc and the syllable count for each stanza is six for the first line, three for the second, and eight for the third, six for the fourth, three for the fifth, and eight for the sixth.

Triolet

An eight-lined poem where the first line is repeated in the fourth and seventh lines, the second line is repeated in the final line, and only the first two end-words are used to rhyme. With capital letters indicating repeated lines, the rhyme scheme looks like ABaAabAB.

Triquain

A seven-lined poem with three syllables on the first line, six on the second, nine on the third, 12 on the fourth, nine on the fifth, six on the sixth, and three on the seventh. Multiple triquains can be put together.

Triquint

A 15-lined poem divided into three stanzas of five lines each. Lines three and four of stanza one repeat in stanza two and 3. Each stanza has nine syllables for the first line, seven for the second, five for the third, three for the fourth, and one syllable for the fifth. The rhyme scheme is a,a,A1,A2,b / a,a,A1,A2,b / a,a,A1,A2,b.

Triversen

An 18-lined poem broken into tercets (three-lined stanzas). Each tercet is a single sentence with two to four feet (collections of stressed and unstressed syllables) per line.

Trochee

A collection of two or more quatrains (four-lined stanzas)
with rhyme scheme abcb or abab. The 24 syllables per
stanza are broken into seven syllables on the first line, five
on the second, seven on the third, and five on the fourth.
Each line begins with a stressed syllable and alternates
between stressed and unstressed syllables.

Trois-par-Huit

An eight-lined poem broken into three sections. The
sections are divided into a group of three lines first
followed by either another group of three lines or two lines.
The tercet or couplet you don't use follows the second
stanza. The 60 syllables in the poem are divided into three
syllables in the first line, six in the second, then nine,
followed by twelve, twelve again, then nine, six, and three.
The rhyming pattern is aab / bbc / cc or aab / bb / ccc. The
last line doubles as the title of the poem and summarizes
the poem's meaning.

Tyburn

A six-lined poem with only two syllables on each of the
first four lines and nine syllables for the last two lines. The
first four lines rhyme with each other and are all descriptive
words. The last two lines also rhyme. Additionally, the first
two lines are repeated as the fifth through eighth syllables
of line five, and the third and fourth lines are repeated as
the fifth and eighth syllables of line six.

Vers Beaucoup

A collection of four-lined stanzas. Hidden in the first line are three words that rhyme with each other. The second line contains one word that rhymes with the rhyming word from line one, and two more words that rhyme with each other. The third line contains a word that rhymes with the double-rhyme from the previous line, and its own, separate double-rhyme. Line four follows the same rules as line three. (aaa - line one, abb - line two, bcc - line three, and cdd -line four) The last words of each line are traditionally one of the rhyming words.

Villanelle

A 19-lined poem broken into five, three-lined stanzas and one four-lined stanza. With capitals to represent repeating lines, the rhyme scheme looks like A1,b,A2 / a,b,A1 / a,b,A2 / a,b,A1 / a,b,A2 / a,b,A1,A2.

Wrapped Refrain

A 12-lined poem broken into two, six-lined stanzas. The first four syllables in the first line double as the last four syllables of the sixth line. There are eight syllables on each of the first four lines of the stanzas and twelve syllables for each of the last two lines. The rhyme scheme is aabbcc.

Rhyming Poems

A L'Arora
Alouette
Ballade
Bref Double
CinqTroisDecaLa Rhyme
Compound Word Verse
Con-Verse
Constanza
Decuain
Diatelle
Duo-Rhyme
Florette
Ghazal
Grá Reformata
Gwawdodyn
Harrisham Rhyme
Hexsonnetta
Kyrielle
La Charta
La'ritmo
Lai
Lauranelle
Lento
Loop (see Echo)
Luc Bat
Madrigal
Memoriam
Mini-Monoverse
Minute Poetry
Mirror Sestet
Mirrored Refrain
Monchielle
Monorhyme
Monotetra

Musette
Nove Otto
Octameter
Ottava Rima
Quadrilew
Quatern
Rhyme Royal
Rispetto
Rondeau
Rondel
Rondelet
Roundabout
Sestina
Sonnet, Canzone
Sonnet, English
Sonnet, Italian
Terza Rima
Terzanelle
Tongue Twister
Tri-fall
Triolet
Triquint
Trochee
Trois-par-Huit
Tyburn
Vers Beaucoup
Villanelle
Wrapped Refrain

Non-rhyming Poems

-ing
Abecedarian
Abstract
Alliterisen
Alphabet Poetry
American Sentence
Anagrammatic Poetry
Ballad (see Narrative)
Blank Verse
Blitz
Blues Poem
Bop
Brevette
Cascade
Cento (see Found Poem)
Chant
Cinquain
Clarity Pyramid
Couplet
Diamante
Doggerel
Echo
Epic (see Narrative)
Epigram
Erasure (see Found Poem)
Etheree
Fibonacci
Five Ws
Found Poem
Free Verse
Golden Shovel
Haibun (see Haiku)
Haiga (see Haiku)

Haiku
Hay(na)ku
Joseph's Star
Katauta
Kenning
Lanturne
Limerick
List
Lune
Naani
Narrative
Nonet
Oddquain
Ode (Horatian, Pindaric, Irregular)
Palindrome
Pantoum
Paradelle
Pleiades
Prose Poem
Puente
Quatrain
Quinzaine
Renga
Rictameter
Riddle Poem
Sapphic
Sedoka (see Katauta)
Senryu (see Haiku)
Septolet
Shadorma
Shape
Sijo
Somonka (see Tanka)
Sound
Synchronicity
Tanka

Tetractys
Triquain
Triversen

Syllable-Count Poems

Alliterisen
Alouette
American Sentence
Blank Verse
Bref Double
CinqTroisDecaLa Rhyme
Cinquain
Clarity Pyramid
Compound Word Verse
Con-Verse
Constanza
Decuain
Diatelle
Duo-Rhyme
Etheree
Fibonacci
Florette
Ghazal
Gwawdodyn
Haiga (see Haiku)
Haiku
Joseph's Star
Katauta
La'ritmo
Lai
Lanturne
Lauranelle
Limerick
Luc Bat
Lune
Madrigal
Memoriam
Mini-Monoverse
Minute Poetry

Monchielle
Monotetra
Musette
Naani
Nonet
Nove Otto
Octameter
Oddquain
Ottava Rima
Quadrilew
Quatern
Quinzaine
Renga
Rhyme Royal
Rictameter
Rispetto
Rondeau
Rondel
Rondelet
Roundabout
Sapphic
Sedoka (see Katauta)
Senryu (see Haiku)
Shadorma
Sijo
Somonka (see Tanka)
Sonnet, Canzone
Sonnet, English
Sonnet, Italian
Synchronicity
Tanka
Terzanelle
Tetractys
Tri-fall
Triquain
Triquint

Non-Syllable-Count Poems

-ing
A L'Arora
Abecedarian
Abstract
Alphabet Poetry
Anagrammatic Poetry
Ballad (see Narrative)
Ballade
Blitz
Blues Poem
Bop
Brevette
Cascade
Cento (see Found Poem)
Chant
Couplet
Diamante
Doggerel
Echo
Epic (see Narrative)
Epigram
Erasure (see Found Poem)
Five Ws
Found Poem
Free Verse
Golden Shovel
Grá Reformata
Haibun (see Haiku)
Harrisham Rhyme
Hay(na)ku
Hexsonnetta
Kenning
Kyrielle
La Charta

Lento
List
Loop (see Echo)
Mirror Sestet
Mirrored Refrain
Monorhyme
Narrative
Ode (Horatian, Pindaric, Irregular)
Palindrome
Pantoum
Paradelle
Pleiades
Prose Poem
Puente
Quatrain
Riddle Poem
Septolet
Sestina
Shape
Terza Rima
Tongue Twister
Triolet
Vers Beaucoup
Villanelle

Metered Poems

Blank Verse
Decuain
Duo-Rhyme
Florette
Grá Reformata
Hexsonnetta
La Charta
Lauranelle
Limerick
Madrigal
Memoriam
Minute Poetry
Rhyme Royal
Rispetto
Roundabout
Sapphic
Sonnet, English
Sonnet, Italian
Triversen
Trochee

Line-Count Poems

<u>1-5 lines</u>
American Sentence   1
Somonka (see Tanka) 1
Couplet   2
Florette   2
Blues Poem   3
Brevette   3
Haiga (see Haiku)   3
Haiku   3
Hay(na)ku   3
Katauta   3
Lune   3
Quinzaine   3
Senryu (see Haiku)   3
Sijo   3
Gwawdodyn   4
Loop (see Echo)   4
Memoriam   4
Monotetra   4
Naani   4
Pantoum   4
Quatrain   4
Sapphic   4
Vers Beaucoup   4
Cinquain   5
Lanturne   5
Limerick   5
Oddquain   5
Riddle Poem 5
Tanka   5
Tetractys   5

<u>6-10 lines</u>

<u>11-20 lines</u>

Alouette   12
Cascade   12
Minute Poetry   12
Mirrored Refrain   12
Wrapped Refrain   12
Rondel   13
Bref Double   14
Hexsonnetta   14
Rondel Prime 14
Sonnet, English   14
Sonnet, Italian   14
Compound Word Verse   15
Constanza   15
Diatelle   15
Rondeau   15
Triquint   15
Octameter   16
Quadrilew   16
Quatern   16
La Charta   18
Tri-fall   18
Triversen   18
Terzanelle   19
Villanelle   19
Bop   20
Monchielle   20
Roundabout   20

<u>21-50 lines</u>

Lauranelle   22
Paradelle   24
Synchronicity 24
Grá Reformata   27
A L'Arora   32
La'ritmo   32

Sestina 39
Blitz   50

<u>Unspecified</u>
-ing
Abecedarian
Abstract
Alphabet Poetry
Anagrammatic Poetry
Ballad (see Narrative)
Ballade
Blank Verse
Cento (see Found Poem)
Chant
Doggerel
Echo
Epic (see Narrative)
Epigram
Erasure (see Found Poem)
Five Ws
Found Poem
Free Verse
Golden Shovel
Haibun (see Haiku)
Kenning
List
Luc Bat
Madrigal
Monorhyme
Narrative
Ode (Horatian, Pindaric, Irregular)
Palindrome
Prose Poem
Puente
Renga
Shape

Terza Rima
Tongue Twister

www.ingramcontent.com/pod-product-compliance
Lightning Source LLC
Chambersburg PA
CBHW051921250726
48659CB00002B/775